# CHRISTMAS EVE IN THE DINER

# CHRISTMAS EVE IN THE DINER

## Daily readings for Advent

Thom M Shuman

wild goose
publications  www.ionabooks.com

Copyright © 2017 Thom M Shuman

First published 2017 by
Wild Goose Publications,
21 Carlton Court
Glasgow, G5 9JP, UK
the publishing division of the Iona Community.
Scottish Charity No. SC003794.
Limited Company Reg. No. SC096243.

ISBN 978-1-84952-568-8

cover photo © Daniel M. Cisilino | Dreamstime

The publishers gratefully acknowledge the support of the Drummond Trust, 3 Pitt Terrace, Stirling FK8 2EY in producing this book.

All rights reserved. Apart from the circumstances described below relating to non-commercial use, no part of this publication may be reproduced in any form or by any means, including photocopying or any information storage or retrieval system, without written permission from the publisher.

Non-commercial use: The material in this book may be used non-commercially for worship and group work without written permission from the publisher. If photocopies of small sections are made, please make full acknowledgement of the source, and report usage to the CLA or other copyright organisation.

Thom M Shuman has asserted his right in accordance with the Copyright, Designs and Patents Act, 1988, to be identified as the author of this work.

*Overseas distribution*
*Australia:* Willow Connection Pty Ltd, Unit 4A, 3-9 Kenneth Road, Manly Vale, NSW 2093
*New Zealand:* Pleroma, Higginson Street, Otane 4170, Central Hawkes Bay
*Canada:* Novalis/Bayard Publishing & Distribution, 10 Lower Spadina Ave., Suite 400, Toronto, Ontario M5V 2Z2

Printed by Bell & Bain, Thornliebank, Glasgow

# CONTENTS

| | |
|---|---|
| Introduction | 7 |
| **First week of Advent** | 9 |
| First Sunday of Advent: God of Advent | 11 |
| First Monday of Advent: Tambourine God | 13 |
| First Tuesday of Advent: Builder God | 15 |
| First Wednesday of Advent: Holy God | 17 |
| First Thursday of Advent: Haggai's God | 19 |
| First Friday of Advent: God of the overlooked | 21 |
| First Saturday of Advent: Mothering God | 23 |
| **Second week of Advent** | 25 |
| Second Sunday of Advent: Eye-opening God | 27 |
| Second Monday of Advent: Imaginative God | 29 |
| Second Tuesday of Advent: Generous God | 31 |
| Second Wednesday of Advent: Holy One | 33 |
| Second Thursday of Advent: Valuing God | 35 |
| Second Friday of Advent: Star-casting God | 37 |
| Second Saturday of Advent: Extravagant God | 39 |
| **Third week of Advent** | 41 |
| Third Sunday of Advent: Loving God | 43 |

| | |
|---|---|
| Third Monday of Advent: Home of our lives | 45 |
| Third Tuesday of Advent: God of the insignificants | 47 |
| Third Wednesday of Advent: Blessing God | 49 |
| Third Thursday of Advent: Listening God | 51 |
| Third Friday of Advent: Dancing God | 53 |
| Third Saturday of Advent: Patient God | 55 |
| Fourth week of Advent | 57 |
| Fourth Sunday of Advent: Revealing God | 59 |
| Fourth Monday of Advent: Host of our hearts | 61 |
| Fourth Tuesday of Advent: Accepting God | 63 |
| Fourth Wednesday of Advent: God in community | 65 |
| Fourth Thursday of Advent: Emmanuel | 67 |
| Fourth Friday of Advent: God of joy | 69 |
| Fourth Saturday of Advent: Welcoming God | 71 |
| Christmas Eve: God of the diner | 73 |
| Christmas Day: Interrupting God | 75 |
| Sources and acknowledgements | 78 |

# INTRODUCTION

For most of his life, our son has lived in settings for persons with mental and developmental challenges, which means that we have spent many Christmases on the road, going to visit him and taking him out for a meal on this holy day. Not surprisingly, there aren't many places open on Christmas, and so we have shared a lot of meals with folk in diners. There has always been a wide diversity in the folk who stop in diners on Christmas – singles, older couples, families with squirming kids, truckers, and some who could only afford a cup of coffee. The staff at diners have always been cheerful, welcoming, inviting folk, joining in the Christmas songs and chatting with those who are obviously alone and lonely.

This little book is for all those who find themselves serving, eating, resting and singing in diners (real and metaphorical) in this holy season, and in all the days before and after, in hope that they will discover God there, serving and eating and resting and singing and welcoming them with open arms.

*Thom M Shuman*

# FIRST WEEK OF ADVENT

# FIRST SUNDAY OF ADVENT

*So Boaz took Ruth and she became his wife. When they came together, the Lord made her conceive, and she bore a son … They named him Obed; he became the father of Jesse, the father of David.*

Ruth 4:13,17b (NRSV)

## God of Advent

When I was growing up, and the time came around, I always dreaded the first day of school. We would sit in class and the teacher would start calling the roll. When my name was called there was always this moment of silence after I answered … And then, inevitably, came: 'Are you Mike's brother?' … Or 'Are you Barbara's brother?' And I would give a quick nod, or the simple answer that, yes, Mike (or Barbara) was my older sibling, and the teacher would move on. And so it went … year after year.

When I graduated I couldn't wait to go off to college. Finally, I thought, I would be on my own – finally I would be out of the shadow of my older siblings. And that lasted for a while, about six years in fact. Until I went back to our hometown to work. And then, whenever I would meet someone new, and tell them my name, there'd always be this moment of silence. Followed by, inevitably: 'So, are you James and Steve's brother?' – now referring to my younger siblings!

I wonder if that was how Jesse felt. He apparently grew up to be quite a prosperous rancher and farmer, and had a large family. He became known for his faith and holy ways, so much so that, according to rabbinic tradition, he was one of four people to die without sin. Yet in all those years, Jesse was probably simply known as the grandson of the saintly Ruth and generous Boaz.

In his most successful years, when he should have been best known for who *he* was, he became identified as 'the father of David' – the greatest king of Israel. Talk about living in deep shadows.

We have all lived in someone else's shadow at some time in our lives. A family member, a friend, a partner, a boss, a professor, a coach … We all know what it feels like to be noticed, not for who we are or what we have accomplished, or might accomplish, but for the gifts and achievements of others around us. Does this experience make us more aware of those who live in the shadows today? Can we look past the star of the show and notice the stage crew, the ticket-takers and the parking attendants?

Can we look beyond the glitter of the season and recognise the forgotten on the grimy streets around us?

### Prayer

*Help us to search the shadows for your children, God of Advent,*
*so we may take them by the hand,*
*bring them into the light of hope and grace,*
*honour them for their gifts*
*and recognise them for who they are:*
*your beloved children.*
*Amen*

# FIRST MONDAY OF ADVENT

*Then the prophet Miriam, Aaron's sister, took a tambourine in her hand; and all the women went out after her with tambourines and with dancing. And Miriam sang to them: 'Sing to the Lord, for he has triumphed gloriously; horse and rider he has thrown into the sea.'*

Exodus 15:20–21(NRSV)

## Tambourine God

We just can't seem to help ourselves – we have to analyse, explain and theorise about everything. Something happens in the world, and immediately the experts and talking heads come together and spend hours debating the whys and wherefores, listing the full ramifications and possibilities of the momentous event. A simple task is given to a group of people, and immediately committees and subcommittees are formed and a process begun to come up with goals and objectives, with a final report to be produced with colour-coded pages and all sorts of pie charts and Excel spreadsheets. We just can't seem to help ourselves. This is how we deal with what happens in our lives.

This was true even back in the days of the Bible. God's people are rescued from slavery and brought through the mighty waters to safety, and Moses cannot help himself. This self-proclaimed inarticulate leader suddenly begins to sing a rather lengthy song about the experience. And then, in true human fashion, sits down to explain it all – not just in one book – but five! He just couldn't help himself.

Of course, we could just pick up our tambourines and sing. We could sing a simple song of praise, maybe like one of those Taizé chants which, when sung over and over again, begin to transform our hearts and souls and draw us closer to God. We could join hands with Miriam and the women and children and simply dance with joy to celebrate all the wonders, goodness, hope and life God has given us. We could spin and whirl and laugh until we fall to the ground in exhaustion and gaze up at the infinite beauty of the night sky – blazing and bursting with stars and moons. We could ... But that's not how we deal with what happens in our lives, is it?

Prayer

*We could spend this season talking, debating, analysing*
*what exactly happened when and where and how;*
*or we could take your hand, Tambourine God,*
*and learn the dance steps of grace and joy*
*you long to teach us.*
Amen

# FIRST TUESDAY OF ADVENT

*Then little children were being brought to him in order that he might lay his hands on them and pray. The disciples spoke sternly to those who brought them; but Jesus said, 'Let the little children come to me, and do not stop them; for it is to such as these that the kingdom of heaven belongs.'*

Matthew 19:13–14 (NRSV)

## Builder God

On my way home from work every day I pass a busy construction site where large machines are moving around great piles of dirt, digging great holes and transporting pipes and lumber from place to place – something big is being built, something new is going up, but there is no signage indicating exactly what is taking place.

Against the immense drama of the construction the other day, I noticed them: a father sitting on the sidewalk with his child standing next to him and an empty stroller beside. The little one was absolutely mesmerised with all the activity going on. The movement, the noise, the sheer enormity of the dancing machinery had them both enthralled. Then I could see the child lean over to her dad and say something, and the father reply, while pointing out something in the distance.

I wonder if that's what Jesus was doing with the kids who were brought to him.

They'd ask him about what was happening, and Jesus would sit down beside them and point out things like God moving governments and history around so that the kingdom of justice could be built; to holes deep enough to hold all our foolishness; to shelters for the homeless and forgotten being erected; to weapons being broken and converted into garden implements …

'The day is coming,' Jesus would whisper to the kids, 'when the poor will be welcomed at the wedding feasts, when the forgotten will be remembered, when children will be heard and not just overlooked – when hope will overcome despair, gentleness will replace bitterness and love will be preferred over hate.'

Something big is being built, something new is going up. Can we become kids again, and stop to wonder?

Prayer

*As you continue to construct your kingdom*
*in our midst, Builder God,*
*hand us the tools and gifts*
*we need to help.*
*Amen*

# FIRST WEDNESDAY OF ADVENT

*Epaphras, who is one of you, a servant of Christ Jesus, greets you. He is always wrestling in his prayers on your behalf, so that you may stand mature and fully assured in everything that God wills.*

Colossians 4:12 (NRSV)

## Holy God

Epaphras, that's who did it, that is who sent the cards.

Ten years ago, when we were on our traumatic journey through the legal system with our son Teddy, we received literally hundreds of cards, e-mails and calls from folk all over the world, speaking of their concern and love for all of us. These messages meant so much.

But each and every day, without fail, one of the green cards showed up in our mailbox. Cards which had a biblical verse of hope and support, of encouragement and compassion printed on them. Cards which reminded us that God always whispers grace and peace to us, even when we are too angry to talk with God; that when we stand knee-deep in despair, we are not alone; that when we are too exhausted to even get out of bed, someone else, somewhere, is lifting us up to God.

We never found out who sent those cards; we probably never will. I simply call her or him Epaphras: that person who wrestled in prayer every day on our behalf so that we could stand again when we fell down, so we could heal when we were most broken, so we could be assured that in everything, every moment, God was with us.

**Prayer**

*Help us to be the Epaphras that another needs.*
*With a simple card, a note,*
*we can remind others of your grace, your love,*
*your life in them, Holy God,*
*so they might continue to discover you in the silence,*
*the pain, the grief,*
*the questions of their lives.*
*Amen*

# FIRST THURSDAY OF ADVENT

*Who is left among you that saw this house in its former glory? How does it look to you now? Is it not in your sight as nothing?*

Haggai 2:3 (NRSV)

## Haggai's God

It was only a short-term contract, the manager at Temp Prophets, told Haggai. It probably wouldn't last longer than six months, so don't sweat it. Just put in the hours, do what you're told and report back for the next posting.

Which is precisely what Haggai did. He went, took care of the job, and came back to his obscure life after the contract ran out. No wonder his little book is stuck towards the end of the Old Testament; no wonder his words are rarely heard in church; no wonder people ask: 'What in the world does some old dead guy named Haggai have to do with us?'

Yet in the midst of his obscurity, in the middle of his forgotten words, come some key questions which resonate with all generations:

Why do we obsess so much about the past? Why do we keep talking about the good old days, as if there's been nothing since that can compare to this mythological era?

Why do we insist that the church can/will only be successful once we, once again, have three services in the morning (and one in the evening) and a Sunday School programme with 1000 kids (and only 3 teachers)?

In just a few short months, Haggai caught on to what God was trying to do. Not build an exact replica of the past, but create a dynamic *new* community.

Not live in the state of what used to be, but form a new people, including those we least expect. Not have us sit around the table at night, as the crumbs of the dinner are licked off the floor by the dog, the last of the wine is poured out and we tell the same old stories over and over again – but point our eyes out the window, where the new day, the new life, our future with God, is just beginning to dawn.

Prayer

*Help us to stop obsessing about the past, Haggai's God,*
*so we might catch a glimpse*
*of what you are doing right now*
*in our midst.*
*Amen*

# FIRST FRIDAY OF ADVENT

*After the Sabbath, as the first day of the week was dawning, Mary Magdalene and the other Mary went to see the tomb.*

Matthew 28:1 (NRSV)

## God of the overlooked

Some years ago there was a TV comedy with a cast of characters that included three guys who would inevitably come into the scene. The fellow in the middle always introduced themselves in this way: 'Hi, I'm Larry, this is my brother Darryl, and this is my other brother Darryl.' Of course we were never given a clue as to what the 'the other Darryl' did or who he was.

We really don't know who 'the other Mary' was either, but obviously she didn't have the same 'star quality' as Mary Mags. Some say she was given this title because Mary was such a common name back then. Some believe she was the sister of Mary, the mother of Jesus. Some posit she was married to Alphaeus, and that their son was the disciple James (who was known by a similar 'title': James the Little/Less – as if he, too, was of little consequence in the grand scheme of things).

We don't know what 'the other Mary' did either. Maybe she simply made sure the folk following Jesus were fed and looked after, coming around after them and picking up their dirty clothes.

Maybe she was the one who always made creative excuses for Jesus when he'd disappeared and everyone was looking for him, never revealing the fact that he'd gone off to recharge his spiritual batteries.

Maybe she was the one who kept refilling Andrew's cup, while patiently listening to his plaintive, 'Peter! All everyone ever talks about is Peter! He wouldn't even know Jesus if I hadn't introduced them …'

We don't know why she is even mentioned. But perhaps it is simply a recognition by the Gospel writers of a woman who was always there when someone needed her, and always overlooked when they didn't. Just like some folk we know.

Prayer

*Open our eyes to those who look after us, God of the overlooked:*
*those who listen to us,*
*those who simply go about their ministry of caring,*
*giving and loving.*
Amen

# FIRST SATURDAY OF ADVENT

*But the midwives feared God; they did not do as the king of Egypt commanded them, but they let the boys live.*

Exodus 1:17 (NRSV)

## Mothering God

They had absolutely no power.

No one was going to come to their defence.

No one would be willing to stand at their side.

So, why did Shiphrah and Puah do it; why were they willing to risk their lives (and perhaps the lives of their families and friends); why did they dare to defy the most powerful ruler of their time?

Why? …

Because it is precisely when despair roams our hearts
that we need to midwife hope;

it is precisely when the bullies stand over little children
that we need to midwife courage;

it is precisely when the power-hungry gain control
that we need to midwife resistance;

it is precisely when the arrogant tell us that only *they* can save us
that we need to midwife trust in God;

it is precisely in this moment, as in every moment,
in our communities, as in every place,
that we must midwife the spirit of Shiphrah and Puah,
so grace, peace, life continue to be birthed
when we most need them.

Prayer

*You call us to be midwives, Mothering God,*
*not because we are strong and courageous,*
*but because you can use our vulnerability*
*and hope*
*if we but trust in you,*
*in every moment,*
*in every place.*
*Amen*

# SECOND WEEK OF ADVENT

# SECOND SUNDAY OF ADVENT

*So Ananias went and entered the house. He laid his hands on Saul and said, 'Brother Saul, the Lord Jesus, who appeared to you on your way here, has sent me so that you may regain your sight and be filled with the Holy Spirit.'*

Acts 9:17 (NRSV)

## Eye-opening God

Every church wants to grow. Every pastor wants to be able to bring in new people.

But what happens when the most progressive church in town is visited by the most conservative voice in the community, who gives every indication that *this* is the family of faith she has been searching for and finally feels she has found?

How does the pastor who takes pride in looking after folk on the streets – making sure they are fed, battling city leaders to open more shelters for longer hours – respond when two of the street families show up and announce they want to be baptised and join the church?

What does the seminary student, who all the professors are convinced is destined for one of the tall-steeple churches coveted by so many in the denomination, do when she opens the letter from the tiny, struggling, destined-to-close-its-doors congregation telling her that they believe God is calling her to serve with them at the corner of Hopeless and Washed Out?

Maybe these are the moments, the people, the challenges we are offered to help us regain our sight and see the kingdom as it is truly meant to be.

**Prayer**

*Remind us, Eye-opening God,
that the people you send us to care for
(and care for us)
may not always be the ones
we expect.
Amen*

# SECOND MONDAY OF ADVENT

*Greet one another with a holy kiss. All the churches of Christ greet you.*
Romans 16:16 (NRSV)

## Imaginative God

This simple little verse follows a long list of folk towards the end of a letter to the believers in Rome. It doesn't have the great theological implications of chapters 4 and 5; it doesn't resound with the high notes of chapter 8; it isn't urging folk to a new lifestyle like chapter 12, but this often overlooked part of the letter tells us something very important about the early church.

Paul mentions women as well as men. He speaks of individuals as well as faith communities. He tells of those who have been imprisoned with him, as well as those who supported him in his journeys and ministry of spreading the gospel – he calls them friends, co-workers, relatives. There are Jews and Gentiles, Greeks, Romans, Asians. Rich and poor, young and old. Paul considers them all to be saints; not because they are more pious than others, but because they are believers, just like you and me.

They are the constant reminders that the early church was a diverse community which welcomed people from every culture, every background, every economic status, every level of education, every sort of work … Folk who lived out the good news that Jesus came for *all people*, not just a few, that the church is the household of everyone, not just the privileged, that faith is shared and learned from every imaginable person.

They are us, or could be us … if we just dared.

## Prayer

*Like the folk behind the scenes of a play, Imaginative God,
it is often those no one sees
who actually make something special happen –
in our churches, in our world, in our lives.
So we give thanks for them,
even as we try to open our eyes to notice them.
Amen*

# SECOND TUESDAY OF ADVENT

*A centurion there had a slave whom he valued highly, and who was ill and close to death.*

Luke 7:2 (NRSV)

## Generous God

How much do we value those who serve us?

The person who cuts our hair, and asks us how things are going, and what we're doing today, do we ask them about their work, their family, what might be happening in their life too? The server/waiter at a meal with colleagues or friends: do we notice the dark circles under her eyes, the way she stretches to get the kinks out of her back, the worry lines on the forehead of someone too young to carry such burdens? The young man who gets up every morning to deliver the newspaper in the dark and damp; the bus driver who picks up our kids or grandkids; the person who works on our car; the lady who speaks a different language who cleans and tidies our hotel room ... how much do we value those who serve us?

One of the jobs I had to pay my way through college was as a cook in a restaurant. I know the long hours that are put in, the incredible amount of time spent on one's feet, and the feeling of caring for customers who seem to care for nothing but themselves. And I know how much I was paid (not a whole lot).

But I also got to know the servers. I saw them berated because there wasn't enough ice in a drink, hollered at because a knife was dirty, rudely waved at by someone who thought he was a VIP (but was really being a JERK).

I got to know how much the servers were paid, which was less than me. I heard their stories of trying to feed and clothe kids on subsistence wages, which meant they relied on the gratuities, only to see a group of businessmen, who had just spent several hundred on a meal, drop two dollars on the table. I have seen folk pull out calculators to figure out (to the penny) what each person owed on the bill, and then walk away leaving the server with nothing but a table to clean.

How much do we value those who serve us?

As much as this nameless centurion?

Or less?

### Prayer

*May we honour those who serve us, Generous God,*
*and become free to walk Christ's way.*
*Amen*

# SECOND WEDNESDAY OF ADVENT

## Holy One

I admit it. I'm more minor than major when it comes to this holy season.

Me, I'll take the simple Advent wreath over the Christmas tree. I'll take the purple and pink candles over 40,000 lights flashing from every house. I'll take silence over the din of commercials. And I'll take sitting and waiting in the shadows, over the stress and strain of wandering from brightly lit store to brightly lit store to shopping mall …

For some folk it isn't Christmas until they sing or hear 'O holy night' or 'O come, all ye faithful' or 'Joy to the world' or the (overly used) 'Hallelujah chorus'. But it has always been the minor-key pieces that speak to me. I could sing 'In the bleak midwinter' every time in worship. Part of it has to do with the incredibly moving words of Christina Rossetti. But it is also the musical dissonance which speaks to me, reflecting the tension which hangs in the air at this time of year; the clash and discordancy of celebrating the Child born into poverty with opulent gift-giving, of feasting and throwing away food while so many lives are growing emptier and emptier.

Perhaps that is why, in this season where every time we gather for worship we hear from Isaiah, I turn to the minor-key prophets. Folk like Habakkuk, who don't get the glory and honour of being read every Christmas, but who, in the hectic moments which assail us, use moving words to speak of the time we should await; who remind us of the God whose one desire is to love us, even while we believe that love is a commodity to be bought and sold.

A professor in seminary told a story about a Presbyterian pastor in the Shenandoah Valley during the American Civil War, an area which was utterly devastated as the battles raged. During a particularly tough time, after one of the armies moving through had taken all the food, crops and livestock, leaving the people with practically nothing, the pastor stood up on a Sunday morning and read from the Book of Habakkuk (3:17–18, NRSV):

*Though the fig tree does not blossom*
*and no fruit is on the vines;*
*though the produce of the olive fails*
*and the fields yield no food;*
*though the flock is cut off from the fold*
*and there is no herd in the stalls,*
*yet I will rejoice in the Lord;*
*I will exult in the God of*
*my salvation.*

In every bleak midwinter, the prophet Habakkuk reminds us: God is with us.

### Prayer

*In the silence of this season,*
*in the discord of our lives,*
*continue to walk with us, Holy One.*
*Amen*

# SECOND THURSDAY OF ADVENT

*'Do not regard your servant as a worthless woman, for I have been speaking out of my great anxiety and vexation all this time.'*

1 Samuel 1:16 (NRSV)

## Valuing God

I minored in history while at college so know the reality of who gets to write it. It is the 'winners'; it is those with the power. Or at least that's how it seems. Which is probably why we have 1st and 2nd Samuel, but no 1st and 2nd Miriam; why we have 1st and 2nd Kings, but no histories of the common people; why we have the letters of Peter, James and Paul, but no letters by Phoebe.

I wonder what it would be like to read 1st and 2nd Hannah. Instead of stories about priests, perhaps we would hear more about women who struggled with infertility, or with seeing so many of their babies die before age one. Instead of long lists of kings, many of whom obviously didn't have a clue as to what they should be doing, we would hear of the poor, who were doing everything they could to put food on the table and care for their families, to seek to be faithful to their God. Instead of generals and battles, maybe we would have been told more stories about the most vulnerable of that day, those forgotten or overlooked in the hurry to win one's status as a great warrior. Maybe we would have more stories about folk like us.

Perhaps if we did have histories written by the women, if we had gospels as seen through the eyes of children, if we had more letters sent by the oppressed and forsaken, we would have caught on a lot quicker that the God we worship

– the One whose birth we celebrate this season, the Spirit which seeks to infuse us with mercy and peace – is on the side of the poor and those we dismiss as worthless – and is longing for us to join in the struggle to end injustice.

Prayer

*Valuing God,*
*help us to listen to the stories,*
*to the lives,*
*to the hearts*
*of all those around us.*
*Amen*

# SECOND FRIDAY OF ADVENT

*And they came, everyone whose heart was stirred, and everyone whose spirit was willing, and brought the Lord's offering to be used …*

Exodus 35:21 (NRSV)

## Star-casting God

It's one of those moments which should be remembered in brilliant colours, with loud dramatic music composed by John Williams and hundreds of thousands watching from massive grandstands. But it is a grainy, flickering, black-and-white image on a very small screen we recall. There were muted voices and silent prayers as the rocket left the ground, then a simple muttered 'Godspeed' as John Glenn became the first American to orbit the earth. It's an all too brief memory of a transformative moment in history.

John Glenn, who died recently at age 95, came back a hero. So much of one that the President issued a secret order forbidding him from flying again for fear of losing this icon. So Glenn dedicated the rest of his life to public service; to becoming one of those people others knew they could count on in the tough moments. He became the epitome of courage; and whenever people thought of the space programme, his face came to mind.

But what about the folk who put him atop that rocket? The ones who helped him to put on his spacesuit, to squeeze into that tiny Mercury capsule? What about the women and men who designed the computers, gadgets and gizmos, came up with the formulas for the fuel? What about the people who built the gantry, who assembled the rocket, who riveted the seams? What about all those whose hearts had been stirred when they first looked at the stars as a kid; whose spirits were willing to spend long, lonely hours in labs in pursuit of dreams everyone laughed at; those people who spent days in libraries studying chemistry, physics, calculus and other things so many of us find too complicated, simply in order that one person might fulfil the dreams of others? They didn't get the ticker-tape parade. They didn't get the interviews on TV. They didn't get the public adulation and honours that came John Glenn's way.

No, they simply went about their jobs. Offering their hearts, their minds, their spirits, their lives in the age-old dream of reaching out to the stars. We don't know their names, we don't remember their achievements, we don't honour them on their passing. But without them, John Glenn would not have been the hero he became.

Without the unnamed and forgotten who are all around us, students would not be taught, patients would not be nursed, the hungry would not be fed, the homeless would not be sheltered.

Prayer

*In a world that honours the individual, Star-casting God,*
*help us to join with and celebrate everyone*
*who simply dreams, reaches, serves,*
*cares for those around them.*
*Amen*

# SECOND SATURDAY OF ADVENT

*While he was at Bethany in the house of Simon the leper, as he sat at the table, a woman came with an alabaster jar of very costly ointment of nard, and she broke open the jar and poured out the ointment on his head. But some were there who said to one another in anger, 'Why was this ointment wasted in this way? For this ointment could have been sold for more than three hundred denarii, and the money given to the poor.' And they scolded her.*

Mark 14:3–5 (NRSV)

## Extravagant God

Who did she think she was?

Of course she was scolded. And we would have done far worse. We would have taken a picture of her foolishness and posted it instantly. We would have shamed her on every form of social media we could find, until she would have to slink off, move to another town, assume a new identity.

We wouldn't be that wasteful, would we? Who do people think we are?

Given a gift of great value, receiving a donation of supplies unexpectedly, blessed with a cheque we did not expect – we wouldn't waste it, would we? We would immediately convert or transfer or cash it and give it all to the poor, wouldn't we? …

… unless the boiler needed repair
… unless the rainy day fund needed to be replenished
… unless new choir robes could be bought
… unless the budget needed to be balanced …

Who did she think she was?

God breaking open grace and pouring it all over us in that baby born in Bethlehem?

Prayer

*May we become more wasteful folk these days, Extravagant God,*
*pouring out peace, hope and inclusion*
*into a world in which such things are*
*in scarce supply.*
*Amen*

# THIRD WEEK OF ADVENT

# THIRD SUNDAY OF ADVENT

*But Moses' hands grew weary; so they took a stone and put it under him, and he sat on it. Aaron and Hur held up his hands, one on one side, and the other on the other side; so his hands were steady until the sun set.*

Exodus 17:12 (NRSV)

## Loving God

Who held up Hur's hands?

She was the CEO of a leading corporation. She sat on boards of city leadership, business consortiums and local charities. When critical decisions needed to be made, when mayors/senators/governors needed a listening ear, she was the one called.

One day, in a conversation in her office, we talked about her responsibilities, her challenges; what it was like to be so close to power – to be a part of the power. The stresses and strains of being an important player were evident in her face and voice. At one point, her administrative assistant came in with some papers for her to sign. As he was leaving, she looked at me and nodding towards him simply said, 'He's the one who "holds up *my* hands".'

We all know the major players in the political, economic, cultural and religious groups. And we know of the folk who advise and assist the different leaders. We don't use such language, but they are the Hurs of our time. The ones who make it possible for folk to keep steady and do the work they have been called to do.

But who looks after Hur? Who holds up her hands; who supports and steadies him?

We focus so much on those in front of the cameras, at the head tables, in the lead cars of the parades; and so, we never see the partner who provides the safe haven, the kids who keep the parent grounded, the neighbours who look after the yard, the friends who keep Hur from getting too big a head.

Who 'holds up your hands' and keeps you steady?

### Prayer

*Help us to notice the hands which support us,*
*which encourage us,*
*which pray for us,*
*which caress us, Loving God,*
*so we may thank them*
*and hold up theirs as well.*
*Amen*

# THIRD MONDAY OF ADVENT

*May the Lord grant mercy to the household of Onesiphorus, because he often refreshed me and was not ashamed of my chain; when he arrived in Rome, he eagerly searched for me and found me ...*

2 Timothy 1:16–17 (NRSV)

## Home of our lives

A friend once told me a story about a foolish stunt he and some friends had pulled in high school. Nothing dangerous, nothing really lawbreaking. Just the sort of thing that teenage boys do. Living in a small village where everyone knew everybody else, pretty soon the sheriff showed up at the diner to escort the boys to his offices.

When they got there, my friend was allowed to call home.

'Dad,' he began, and stopped, not sure of what to say.

'Where are you, son?'

'Dad, I have been pretty foolish, and ...'

'Son, where are you?'

'Dad, I am so, so sorry. I don't know what got into me ...'

'Son, you don't understand. I don't care what you've done. Where are you? I am coming to get you and bring you home.'

This is the season where God simply says to us, 'I am coming to bring you home.'

### Prayer

*May we be the ones who show others*
*the way to your heart, Home of our lives,*
*even as others have helped us find*
*that road.*
*Amen*

# THIRD TUESDAY OF ADVENT

*These are the names of the twelve apostles: first, Simon, also known as Peter, and his brother Andrew; James son of Zebedee, and his brother John; Philip and Bartholomew; Thomas and Matthew the tax collector; James son of Alphaeus, and Thaddaeus; Simon the Cananaean, and Judas Iscariot, the one who betrayed him.*

Matthew 10:2–4 (NRSV)

## God of the insignificants

Sung to the tune of 'Rudolph, the red-nosed reindeer':

*'You know Andrew and Peter,
James and John,
Philip and Matt,
Judas and Tom,
but do you recall
the most insignificant disciple of all? …'*

(Yes, I know that's *not* how it goes.)

But the truth is there are those disciples about whom we know very, very little. Oh, the big names: Peter, John, Matthew – the ones who got to go on the book tours and appear on all the talk shows; Thomas, who didn't know the way and was obviously from the Show-me school; and Judas, the traitor, the guy who kissed Jesus on the cheek and then kicked him over to the authorities – we know all these folk. Their backgrounds, their families, their work. They have churches and schools, hospitals and colleges, even cities named after them.

But James the Little or the Less (depending on who knew him)? Thad? Simon the Cananaean? Who are these guys? What did they ever accomplish? Truth is, we don't know. They're mentioned once, maybe twice, and then disappear from the stage. Their later lives are shrouded in mystery, legend, speculation. They are forgotten, dismissed, lost.

They didn't write any books and become big successes. But maybe they were the ones walking the streets, taking care of the folk who lived in the shadows.

They didn't appear before crowds of thousands with megawatt smiles on their faces. But maybe they were the ones making sure kids who needed a meal, or a schoolbook, or healthcare got those things.

They weren't the ones the media contacted when they needed a 'faith representative' to come on the morning show. But maybe they were the ones the mother with the addicted child, the dad needing his car repaired, the lonely teenager all trusted, certain that if they knocked on Thad's or Simon the Cananaean's door – they would find a friend.

Maybe, just maybe, they weren't so insignificant after all.

Prayer

*Remind us, God of the insignificants,*
*that a cup of water*
*sometimes goes a lot further in helping others*
*than a mighty ocean of words and good intentions.*
*Amen*

# THIRD WEDNESDAY OF ADVENT

*Now the woman was a Gentile, of Syrophoenician origin. She begged him to cast the demon out of her daughter. He said to her, 'Let the children be fed first, for it is not fair to take the children's food and throw it to the dogs.' But she answered him, 'Sir, even the dogs under the table eat the children's crumbs.' Then he said to her, 'For saying that, you may go – the demon has left your daughter.'*

Mark 7:26–29 (NRSV)

## Blessing God

This is one of those passages folk, especially preachers, wish could be clipped out of the Gospels. It simply doesn't present Jesus in a very favourable light. Which is probably why folk, especially preachers, come up with all sorts of rationalisations for this story: Jesus was having a bad day; Jesus hadn't slept very well; Jesus was focused on something else; Jesus believed his primary role then was to serve his Jewish friends and neighbours, not outsiders. Any and all of these might be valid.

But I think the reason folk, especially preachers, wish this story wasn't in the Gospels is because it doesn't present *us* in a very good light.

A family shows up in distress, and we give them a $20 gift card to send them on their way, rather than take time to listen to their story. Churches collect food baskets at Thanksgiving and Christmas, but figure the same recipients can fend for themselves the other 11 months of the year. We collect supplies for kids at the start of the school year, and then vote down laws that would support their education …

Because we have the whole loaf, we don't realise how important 'crumbs' can be in the lives of our sisters and brothers. With enough crumbs, a family can be fed; with enough crumbs, a home can be built; with enough crumbs, lives can be rebuilt.

### Prayer

*When we are tempted to*
*sweep up the crumbs of your gifts, Blessing God,*
*and toss them in the bin,*
*remind us of how they might offer*
*new life and hope to others.*
*Amen*

# THIRD THURSDAY OF ADVENT

*I, Tertius, the writer of this letter, greet you in the Lord.*

Romans 16:22 (NRSV)

## Listening God

Some people think Tertius actually wrote this letter. Others think he had some notes and sermon scraps from Paul and assembled it from that. Some think he was Paul's amanuensis (your word for the day).

Tertius' name, which means 'third', was a common one for slaves, so he may have been one of Phoebe's servants, sent by his benefactor to help Paul.

We don't really know anything or any more about Tertius beyond this one line. After that, he simply disappears into the mists of history: only a tagline at the end of a book that has transformed churches and lives.

Forgotten.

Probably Tertius was the conduit, the communicator, the intermediary who put Paul in touch with the good folk in Rome, as well as us. Like one of those operators at old telephone switchboards who would receive your call, and then connect you with the person or store you wanted to reach.

Bill was our conduit, our communicator, our intermediary for years when we lived in Cincinnati and would call to speak to our son Teddy. 'Grounds, Bill!' would come his enthusiastic and generous welcome when we called the main number. He would always first ask us how we were doing, and then connect us with Teddy.

When we started driving up every week, Bill was usually the one working at Grounds, where we would first take a pit stop, before heading over to pick up Teddy for an outing.

Bill was big and gruff, but gentle as a lamb. It didn't matter what the weather – he always wore an Hawaiian shirt, and if the temperature was above the teens, usually had shorts on. Bill always wore his graciousness, his joy of life, his compassion on his sleeve, so we always enjoyed the few minutes we'd go to see and talk with him. And it was a special treat for us if Bill had his dogs with him, which he often did, giving us the opportunity to love them and receive their unconditional love.

When we moved to Columbus, we didn't see Bill as much, but still heard his voice on the phone, still bathed in his warmth when he answered.

The other morning Bill went out on his back deck to let his dogs out. And that is where his partner found him, sadly silenced by a fatal heart attack. We will no longer hear his gruff and generous voice, no longer hear about his dogs, no longer be warmed by his spirit.

But Bill will not be lost in the mists of our history, or forgotten.

Prayer

*We give thanks for those good and generous folk, Listening God,*
*who make it possible for us to be connected with*
*family, friends, neighbours, you.*
*Amen*

# THIRD FRIDAY OF ADVENT

*Look! On the mountains the feet of one who brings good tidings, who proclaims peace!*

Nahum 1:15a (NRSV)

## Dancing God

In tiny dancers
celebrating the
Birth on Christmas
Eve;

in the shuffled steps
of the fellow
leading the granddaughter
he raised solo
out on to the dance floor
at her wedding;

in the freezing extremities
of the runners, walkers,
wheelers, bikers
raising money for
medical research
on a wintry day;

in prophets
who walked lonely
paths often wondering

if they were speaking
only to the wind,

peace comes leaping
into our lives!

### Prayer

*May we no longer be wallflowers, Dancing God,*
*but dare to step out on the dance floor*
*of justice and hope with you.*
*Amen*

# THIRD SATURDAY OF ADVENT

*Bind up the testimony, seal the teaching among my disciples. I will wait for the Lord, who is hiding his face from the house of Jacob, and I will hope in him.*

Isaiah 8:16–17 (NRSV)

## Patient God

When the crowd is rushing
to get to the malls,

when the television
overflows with adverts,

when the songs
on the radio come
one right after the other
with no silence in between,

I will wait.

When fear sings a lullaby
to my faith,

when worry nibbles at the edges
of my soul,

when doubt becomes a worn slipper
I ease my feet into,

I will hope.

I will wait,
I will hope …

**Prayer**

*Do you hope we will catch up with you, Patient God,
up ahead, waiting to show us
the way to grace?
Amen*

# FOURTH WEEK OF ADVENT

# FOURTH SUNDAY OF ADVENT

*When the angels had left them and gone into heaven, the shepherds said to one another, 'Let us go now to Bethlehem and see this thing that has taken place, which the Lord has made known to us.'*

Luke 2:15 (NRSV)

## Revealing God

I wonder who got left behind. Maybe it was the old guy dozing by the fire, but with ears like a hawk. Maybe the youngest one, the kid who hadn't had his first job evaluation yet, drew the shortest stick. Maybe it was the shepherdess, simply because of the 'ess' at the end of her position description. But someone got left behind with all the sheep. After all, no self-respecting shepherd would leave his flocks unattended, unprotected – even if God had made something 'known to them'. After all, the angels didn't say, 'Go! Don't worry, we'll stay here and keep an eye on everything.'

We are so enamoured with the mythological, greeting card, Christmas Eve homily setting, aren't we? There is sweet baby Jesus, the Holy Child who never utters a plaintive wail. There is virginal Mary with her pristine-white robe and perfectly coiffed hair. There is sturdy Joseph, leaning on his staff, gently smiling down at the Currier & Ives picture. There are the animals: 1 cow, 4 sheep, 2 donkeys and maybe a curious cat up in the rafters. We are so enamoured with this image, we forget the ones who were left behind.

Just as we forget the ones around us who are left at their posts when everyone else is celebrating Christmas, attending parties, gathering with the family around the tree. We don't have to work, we can take the time off, we can enjoy the holiday break, so we don't notice the ones who are still up on the hillside keeping watch.

The 911 dispatcher, the volunteer at the suicide prevention hotline, the firefighter pulling the 12-hour shift on Christmas Eve, the tow truck driver yanking cars out of ditches, the nurse sitting at the bedside of a little girl in ICU – do we notice them, remember them?

The security guards at my college were a mixed bag of folk. Some spent time getting to know us and letting us know them, some kept their distance. But they were always around, always on the job, usually ignored or forgotten.

One year, I spent the holiday break on campus, working to earn money for the next semester. Christmas Eve found me in my room, listening to music, reading, lonely. There was a knock on the door. When I opened it, there was the security guard who was spending the night looking after the campus, including me. He simply said, 'If you don't have any plans for tomorrow, why don't you come and have Christmas dinner with me and my family?'

The one left behind, the one who drew the short stick, the one usually ignored and forgotten, remembered me!

And I have never forgotten him.

Prayer

*Help us to remember the forgotten around us, Revealing God,*
*and shower them with as much love, attention, compassion*
*as we offer everyone else.*
*Amen*

# FOURTH MONDAY OF ADVENT

*Joseph also went from the town of Nazareth in Galilee to Judea, to the city of David called Bethlehem, because he was descended from the house and family of David. He went to be registered with Mary, to whom he was engaged and who was expecting a child.*

Luke 2:4–5 (NRSV)

## Host of our hearts

They didn't hop the daily shuttle for the quick flight to Bethlehem. They didn't climb aboard the megabus for the trip down. No, they walked. Across rugged, dangerous country. No smooth Isaiah-type holy way for them. It was uphill and downhill and steep both ways. It was hot and dry, then dropped to below freezing at night. They risked encountering wild animals along the way, as well as bandits and others who preyed on the innocent. We aren't told how long it took them, but given the weather, the locale, the pregnancy, it probably took Joseph and Mary at least nine days to walk from Nazareth to Bethlehem, every step more difficult.

We aren't told the details of this journey. But my guess is that, as Joseph and Mary walked, they managed to find places to rest, homes which provided them hospitality, a shelter from the elements, wild animals and bullies. Maybe this was accomplished simply by knocking on the door of the nearest house and looking as bedraggled as possible; maybe it was 'a friend of a friend of a friend said you might be able to put us up for a night' ... Maybe they managed to get the last bed in a local hostel. We don't know.

But I am guessing that, along the way, they encountered hospitality, a welcome from strangers, a good meal and a bed that floated them into safe dreams – all from nameless, forgotten people.

Would we be as willing to take in cold, bedraggled folk knocking at our doors? Would we be gracious enough to offer hospitality to complete strangers?

In an interview I remember, author Madeleine L'Engle was saying she was talking with a friend, a recovering alcoholic, who was planning to drive across country to California. She would be stopping along the way, sometimes in towns where she didn't know a soul. Concerned for her, L'Engle asked her what might happen if she was in a motel room alone, and was suddenly faced with the feeling of wanting to go down to the nearest bar.

'All I would have to do is open the phone book, look up the local chapter of AA,' her friend said, 'and someone would come and be with me until that longing went away.'

Madeleine L'Engle went on to wonder what might happen if *she* was travelling, and found herself in a motel room feeling lonely and fragile. What would the response be, she wondered, if she called up a local pastor saying something along the lines of, 'Hello, I am a Christian, alone and in your town, and I am afraid I may do something that will take me off my journey with Jesus. Can you help?' …

What would the response be? Hospitality, or a cold shoulder?

## Prayer

*If we are lucky,*
*we have encountered such hospitality, Host of our hearts.*
*If we are more fortunate,*
*we are offered the chance to be gracious hosts*
*to folk who need rest, a meal, a friend.*
*Open us to such chances, we pray.*
*Amen*

# FOURTH TUESDAY OF ADVENT

*Philip found Nathanael and said to him, 'We have found him about whom Moses in the law and also the prophets wrote, Jesus son of Joseph from Nazareth.' Nathanael said to him, 'Can anything good come out of Nazareth?' Philip said to him, 'Come and see.'*

John 1:45–46 (NRSV)

## Accepting God

For over 70 years, it's been a classic read and re-read to generations of children and grandchildren. E.B. White's *Stuart Little* is a fantasy novel about a little boy born to human parents who is so tiny that he *'looked very much like a mouse in every way'*. He is tormented by Snowbell, the family cat, but his experiences make him more compassionate. And rather than being the object of embarrassment to his family, he is completely accepted by them for who he is. An outsider, he becomes the central player in this story of hope, love and acceptance.

In the gospels, Jesus is certainly the ultimate outsider. Born into poverty, he never really leaves his village until he begins his ministry. He remarks that he has no place where he can stop and rest. When Philip rushes to tell his friend Nathanael about Jesus, Nathanael cynically dismisses Jesus as an outsider from a nowhere place.

Maybe that's why Jesus was always drawing outsiders to himself. The religious outsider, the ethnic outsider, the gender outsider, the economic outsider, the political outsider – all were welcomed by Jesus, into Jesus' family. He called them to be his disciples, and healed them of their loneliness and illnesses. He invited them to his parties, and accepted their invitations to feast with them. He accepted them for who they were.

Perhaps – because of your country of origin, your family, your job, your gender, your sexual orientation, your economic or educational status – you know what it feels like to be an outsider.

Does this make you more sensitive to the outsiders around you? Does your experience move you to reach out to others?

Do you strive to be the welcome the excluded long to find?

### Prayer

*We are so busy explaining exactly why*
*someone cannot be the person that they claim to be, Accepting God,*
*that we miss the grace,*
*the hope, the life*
*they are longing to share with us.*
*Amen*

# FOURTH WEDNESDAY OF ADVENT

*Now all the tax collectors and sinners were coming near to listen to him. And the Pharisees and the scribes were grumbling and saying, 'This fellow welcomes sinners and eats with them.'*

Luke 15:1–2 (NRSV)

## God in community

For some it's the exchange of Christmas gift lists among family members. For others it's the baking – the cookies, pies and fruitcake. Many cannot wait to go carolling, and there are those for whom the yearly gathering with neighbours does it. But for all of us there is something – a moment, an activity – that says, 'Now – at last – it's Christmas!'

For me, it's the movies. Not the overly violent ones that 'count' because they are set at Christmastime; not every single schmaltzy one; not every animated one. Just certain ones, mostly older, but not always. And there's one common thread to them (and no, it is not Christmas!). It is the common thread of brokenness. There's the single mum working in the corporate world (*Miracle on 34th Street*), the retired general who feels forgotten (*White Christmas*), the husband who thinks he's a failure (*It's a Wonderful Life*), the divorced dad (*The Santa Clause*).

Yet in the midst of all this brokenness, in the midst of all their self-doubts, in their lonely struggles, in their shattered hearts, something happens. A community is formed. Maybe it's a village coming together; maybe it's a reunion of old buddies; maybe it's the love of the fellow in the flat across the hall; maybe it's discovering that, at the heart of all the Christmas hype and stress and worries and fears, it really *does* come down to relationships.

This is the secret to the miracle of the One whose birth we celebrate. He recognised that each and every one of us is broken, and longs to be repaired; he knew that loneliness that walks with each of us in the midst of crowded stores, the fear we all have that we have not achieved what others think we should have (or worse, what *we* think we should have). And he takes those worries, those fears, that loneliness, that longing, that brokenness and creates a community: the family of God. His brothers and sisters aren't the religious leaders, the power brokers, the wealth and the mighty (though they are very welcome); they are the little and the least, the worriers and the weary, the tax collectors and the sinners: you and me.

A community we can find for real, not just in the movies.

### Prayer

*Help us to be the hope,*
*the grace, the love,*
*the welcome others need, God in community.*
*Amen*

# FOURTH THURSDAY OF ADVENT

> *All this took place to fulfil what had been spoken by the Lord through the prophet: 'Look, the virgin shall conceive and bear a son, and they shall name him Emmanuel,' which means "God is with us".*
>
> Matthew 1:22–23 (NRSV)

## Emmanuel

You came,
struggling through
the deep drifts of our sins,
to pull us out,
hand us a warm toddy of grace
and wrap us in
the comfort of
your hope;

you came,
unlatching the storm windows
we have hung over our
hopelessness,
so we can open our hearts
to the bracing breath
of your joy;

you came,
your arms full of groceries,
cooking up a storm,
letting us lick the bowls

and decorate the kitchen
with icing and sprinkles –
then sending us out
with our arms full
of your goodness,
so everyone might
gorge themselves
on your love;

you came,
that little child
taking our hand
on a cold winter night's
walk,
suddenly stopping
and whispering,
'Did you hear that?' …

You came;
and oh how quickly
we
forget!

Prayer

*Take away our Advent-nesia, Emmanuel,*
*so we can see you still with us,*
*in every moment,*
*in every person.*
*Amen*

# FOURTH FRIDAY OF ADVENT

*For God so loved the world ...*
John 3:16 (NRSV)

## God of joy

I have done a lot of weddings over the years. Mostly 20-somethings who are passionately and joyously in love. They are *so much* in love with love that I sometimes want to ask them: 'Do you realise what you are doing? Do you understand the words you are saying? Do you get what the rings symbolise? ... Do you have *any idea* what love is going to cost you?'

Because love is costly. It means becoming more aware of the other than yourself. It means sleepless nights, if you are blessed to have children. It means putting up with the quirks of your partner that drive you crazy. It is recognising that the day may come when the person you danced with in the spring of life now needs to be assisted in a wheelchair. It is knowing that there will be words spoken that are instantly regretted and hurts inflicted that only deep love can mend. It is the awareness that the person you married is constantly changing and surprising you – the great challenge and joy you didn't see coming. And love just might not only break your heart, but take it away completely.

I've got to know a special couple. Old friends and fellow church members, she lost her husband seven years ago, and he, his wife six years back. They know what love can cost.

Yet, the other night, with their kids, grandkids and friends, they said their vows to one another and exchanged rings. I was blessed to be the one presiding as two people decided, no matter what the cost, to love again.

On that night long ago, knowing full well what such love would cost, God became one of us.

**Prayer**

*As you refuse to count the cost*
*but continue to love us, God of joy,*
*may our love become a gift to others.*
*Amen*

# FOURTH SATURDAY OF ADVENT

*And she gave birth to her firstborn son and wrapped him in bands of cloth, and laid him in a manger, because there was no room for them in the inn.*

Luke 2:7 (NRSV)

## Welcoming God

He's a stock character in just about every Christmas pageant. He is the fall guy in many a Christmas Eve sermon. He has become the symbol of the indifferent world into which Jesus was born. Of course I am speaking of the innkeeper. The stocky, bearded, robed figure who has the effrontery to slam the door in the face of the holy family and let them freeze!

But actually, the innkeeper is a mythical character. Our version of what happened that first Christmas is based not so much on what the story tells us, as how the story has been interpreted in songs, sermons, children's plays, movies and books. In reality, there was no inn, and no innkeeper.

The real story has been lost in translation. The Greek in which the Gospel of Luke was written tells us that there was no space available in the 'guest room', not the inn. (Luke uses this same word in describing the place where the Last Supper was held.) Back in those days, houses usually had a guest room in the front. Apparently, Joseph was convinced that a cousin or a friend or an associate would have space for them in their 'guest room'. But with the influx of people into Bethlehem for the census – not a chance. However, each house also had a 'cave' attached to it: the place where the animals were secured at night. And what with the view that the accompanying blood and fluids of childbirth were 'unclean', it probably seemed logical to folk for Mary to be placed in an area that was already messy.

So, no dastardly innkeeper. No cold-hearted rejection of the Christ child. No effrontery to God. Just simple human attempts to make the best of a difficult situation.

After all, what would you do if a family showed up out of the blue on Christmas Eve, and every spare bed, every sofa, every rug was already being used by folk who had already phoned ahead and let you know they were coming?

You would do your best to accommodate them, wouldn't you?

Prayer

*May we become the innkeepers the lonely, the refugee,*
*the ageing, the broken*
*are looking for*
*on this hard journey of life,*
*Welcoming God.*
*Amen*

# CHRISTMAS EVE

*While they were there, the time came for her to deliver her child.*

Luke 2:6 (NRSV)

## God of the diner

They pulled in late at night,
the parking lot overflowing
because it was the only
place open for the holiday;
the dash was blinking
'check engine';
they were running on gas
fumes
and bone-weary from
the long trip;

with calloused, blue-collar
hands, he helped his
baby-coming-at-any-moment
wife out of the pickup
and into the warm diner,
where a couple of
goths offered them
their booth so they
wouldn't be placed on the
45-minutes-at-least
waiting list;

## Christmas Eve in the diner

when her water broke,
the waitresses grabbed towels,
the short-order cook gave the husband
a snort from his hip flask,
and the cop at the end of the counter
delivered the newborn, gently
placing him in a nest
of clean aprons, while
the squeaky-voiced cashier began to
sing 'Silent night', until all joined in:

the stammering introvert,
the burly college student,
the lonely grandparents,
the voiceless teenager signing along;

and in all the commotion,
no one noticed the grizzled
trucker slip the manager
the funds to pay everyone's bill,
as well as a nest egg for
the little one
and his family.

# CHRISTMAS DAY

*In that region there were shepherds living in the fields, keeping watch over their flock by night. Then an angel of the Lord stood before them, and the glory of the Lord shone around them, and they were terrified.*

Luke 2:8–9 (NRSV)

## Interrupting God

Last night we held the traditional Christmas Eve candlelight Communion service – one of the best parts of the church year, one of the best parts of being a pastor. It always follows the same liturgical format, the readings are always the same, except for the psalm, the carols are familiar and beloved, and everything moves towards the moment when we sing 'Silent night' and pass the light of Christ to one another.

But over the years I have learned to always expect some sort of glitch (where did the Christ candle go?), some oversight (what do you mean no one ordered individual candles?), or the scary (a little kid's hair getting singed by leaning too close to the Advent wreath).

Last night proved to be no exception. Just as I started to sit down following the homily, a cell phone blared out: 'If you said something, I didn't understand.' And yes, it got a good laugh, and we moved on with the service.

Yet, I wonder, isn't that our response to the Christmas story, if truth be told?

The angel announces not just good, but the best sort of news – a Saviour has been born: we don't have to depend on our ingenuity, our arrogance, our foolishness to save us from ourselves. 'No,' God announces, 'I will take the burden off your shoulders.' So there is no reason to fear – God or our future. And we basically say, with insistence, that we are quite capable of looking after number one: 'If you said something, I didn't understand.'

The angelic chorus bursts out into a great cantata celebrating this momentous moment in history. 'Wow,' they sing, 'this is great stuff! Peace is being poured out upon all people – you are invited to share it with everyone around you, to see your sister and brother in every person you meet.' And the world responds, as nations decide that it's time to ratchet up the nuclear arms race once again: 'If you said something, we didn't understand.'

The people we usually ignore – the folk who work behind the counters where we eat, the folk who pull our cars out of ditches, the housekeepers who clean our rooms, the folk who mow our lawns – all crowd around us to tell us of the One they have met. The baby born in poverty so we might inherit grace, the little one who shed glory to be swaddled in our fears and worries, the God who chose to become one of us – so we might discover how much we are loved (not hated), how much we are cared for (not forgotten), how much we are welcomed (not rejected) – is in our midst! Those little, least, lost and last of our society go to see – and run back to tell us the good news. And we yawn with our lack of compassion for the most vulnerable: 'If you said something, we didn't understand.'

And yet, however tempting it must be, that is never God's response to us when we cry out for help, when we pray for hope, when we seek God's presence, when we ask for directions once we have left Bethlehem, when we whisper in the loneliness of life's night.

## Prayer

*Continue to whisper to us of grace,*
*to sing of joy and wonder,*
*to shout about the injustices all around us, Interrupting God,*
*until we finally open our hearts and souls to respond,*
*'Now we understand.'*

## SOURCES AND ACKNOWLEDGEMENTS

Bible passages from the NRSV. Passages from NRSV copyright 1989, Division of Christian Education of the National Council of the Churches of Christ in the United States of America. Used by permission. All rights reserved.

Wild Goose Publications, the publishing house of the Iona Community established in the Celtic Christian tradition of Saint Columba, produces books, e-books, CDs and digital downloads on:

- holistic spirituality
- social justice
- political and peace issues
- healing
- innovative approaches to worship
- song in worship, including the work of the Wild Goose Resource Group
- material for meditation and reflection

For more information:

Wild Goose Publications
21 Carlton Court,
Glasgow G5 9JP, UK

Tel. +44 (0)141 429 7281
e-mail: admin@ionabooks.com

or visit our website at
www.ionabooks.com
for details of all our products and online sales